To: Markeyta
Always B
all my love, Marvin O'Neal

EVERYTHING IS GOD

MARVIN O'NEAL

• Chicago •

EVERYTHING IS GOD
MARVIN O'NEAL

Published by
Joshua Tree Publishing
• Chicago •
JoshuaTreePublishing.com

13-Digit ISBN: 978-1-941049-59-4

Photo Credits: Cover Image: ©rolffimages; My Perfect World: ©vovan; Not for Sale: ©Dmitriy; Medicine Vol 1: ©Kevin Carden; Medicine Vol 2: DAISUKE KURASHIMA; Medicine Vol 3: ©peshkova; Not that of Man: ©peshkov

Disclaimer:

Printed in the United States of America

Dedication

To

God the Father who is everything to all, and my daughter who is everything to me.

Mission Statement

The main objective, purpose, and reason I write is to save someone's inner spirit from the penalty of eternal damnation.

Table of Contents

In My Perfect World
By Marvin O'Neal

In My Perfect World

In my perfect world, I would have the perfect girl
No calling the cops on me, no arguments, no quarrels
No baby daddy drama, no cheating in the night
The perfect weight and height, face and type.
In my perfect world, the 7 deadly sins wouldn't exist
No reason for me to put your name on my hitlist
Also known as a getlist, I seek vengeance
But I don't even have to go that route . . . it ended.
In my perfect world, it's all love and no hatred
Real, no fakeness, or being trapped in the matrix
No aggravated assault, public intoxication
Pedophiles, arson, robbery, or rapists.
In my perfect world, there wouldn't be no death
Obituaries, funerals, forever they slept
Never have to grow old, in a nursing home
No assisted living or rotting away in prison.
In my perfect world, there wouldn't be nothing satanic
No evil, no demons roaming through the planet
No roaches, no rats, attack . . . full metal jack
World war combat and that's that
. . . in my perfect world.

In my perfect world, it's no social media
You have to look in a real book . . . forget Wikipedia
No posting messages, videos, or pictures
You want a husband? Go back 40 years and stop fishing.
In my perfect world, not one person is gay
No two dudes holding hands going on their merry way
No girl on girl action, not a drag in sight
Nothing transgender, they on eternal strike.
In my perfect world, racism is brought to an end
The triple K clan would never even begin
No cops taking shots, killing people who look like me
No discrimination or prejudice, because I look like me.
In my perfect world, money wouldn't be needed
You can smoke all you want, so forever stay weeded
It's at the root of all evil, making people sell their souls
It's gone . . . now it's powerless, no control.
In my perfect world, you could see The Most High
Live with The Most High and wouldn't have to ask why
The Judge of all Judges, Father of all
Put your faith in Him, He'll never let you fall
. . . in my perfect world.

In my perfect world, I can drink and never get drunk
No dehydration, hangovers, or sick throwing up
No stumbling and bumbling, or dealing with a D.U.I.
and wouldn't have to worry if I crash and die.
In my perfect world, it's no gangs to gangbang
No blood in blood out and no colors to blame
No 5 or 6 point stars, no lil' homies to train
No tattoos representing whatever set you claim.
In my perfect world, it's no heroin or coke
No cough syrup to drink, or methamphetamine to smoke
It's not 1 pill to pop, no crack to cook
Mary is never leaving, definitely staying put.
In my perfect world, it's no STDs to catch
I could splash any female I want, and straight wreck
Plus . . . it's no diseases, and no viruses to grow
You won't get cancer, I can't even catch a cold.
In my perfect world, it'll never be a war
It's always peace, so aint nothing to fight for
No suicide bombers, no terrorist attacks
Nuclear weapons disappeared and are never coming back
. . . in my perfect world.

In my perfect world, it's no natural disasters
No earthquake destroying the church, killing the pastor
Tsunami waves, washing people away in the field
Volcanoes spitting lava, that spills at will.
In my perfect world, no need for a government
Or a false president, whose best friend is ignorance
Wouldn't be laws to make, bend, or break
Taxes to take, or an economy to regulate.
In my perfect world, there's no prostitution
Sex trafficking turned into a big huge illusion
That tramp couldn't sell her self to my brother on death row
Two cent whore, you gets paid no more.
In my perfect world, it's no internet to use
The web is gone, all cell phones too
Electronic devices, passwords, and all apps
Don't know where you going? Pull out the road map.
In my perfect world, everybody has food
It's Thanksgiving everyday, so mankind is cool
No hunger, no poverty, plenty to go around
Enough to eat . . . for every man, woman, and child
. . . in my perfect world.

In my perfect world, there's no liars or thievery
I'll believe anything you say, because nobody deceiving me
No untruths, never in you is a lying spirit
I'll leave my keys in the truck, windows down, and nobody steals it.
In my perfect world, it wouldn't be time . . . it's timeless
The whole 4th dimension is behind us
Ageless, endless, unending
Undying, non-stop, never ending.
In my perfect world, the laws of physics don't apply
No gravity to keep the stars up in the sky
No force, or energy, which equals no work
No birth, plants won't even grow from the dirt.
In my perfect world, it wouldn't be one problem
From the jungles of the Congo, to the hoods of Harlem
No more problems, dilemmas, or bad news
Bad moods, kill everybody type of attitude.
In my perfect world, I'm perfect and impeccable
Flawless, the very best, exceptional
The highest of the high, greatest of all the greats
Premium supreme, 1st class, 1st rate
. . . in my perfect world.

In my perfect world, my best friend from '79
Wouldn't be on death row. He'd be free, just like me,
But the devil threw a death blow
All life's privileges and one's power have been taken
Now he waiting for the state to cook him like a piece of bacon.
In my perfect world, you need my approval to make a baby
So the epidemic can stop of kids being born crazy
Or delayed with learning, where my daddy at syndrome?
Your mother in the club, instead of being at home.
In my perfect world, I would've been born filthy rich
With a gigantic silver spoon, loaded with money to play with
So much . . . I can swim in a pool of cash 10,000 feet deep
I got enough money to buy all of Wall Street.
In my perfect world, there's no guns to shoot
No pistol to put in your mouth and throw you off the roof
Hand gun, machine gun, kill the whole block with a mini gun
But there's no triggers to pull, I'll have plenty of fun.
In my perfect world, I can shut a woman up with a remote control
Once I push the mute button, they mouth stay closed
No whining or complaining, I don't have to hear that crap
I'll a push the power button and disappear you from the map
. . . in my perfect world.

In my perfect world, I'm Darth Vader, Megatron, Joke
Jason, Freddy . . . Cosa Nostra
Skelator, Candyman to the 7th power
Michael Myers, killing 100 people every hour.
In my perfect world, I'd know telepathy
And read every thought you think, when you aint even next to me
. . . so I see what you're saying, long before you ever say it
I hear everything you tell God before you ever pray it.
In my perfect world, I'd be Jesus Christ
Sacrifice for every human life and give the blind sight
Make sound for the deaf, bless people to speak
Bring you back from the dead, now you're walking the street.
In my perfect world, it's me and two identical twins
We look exactly the same, from the outside in
It's three of us, so my purpose is tripled
To get where we have to get, little by little.
In my perfect world, I'd never be paranoid, unemployed
Or feel like, my life has been destroyed
I'm overjoyed, anything less . . . I avoid
Born on the South Side of Chicago
. . . in my perfect world.

In my perfect world, I'm GOD, I made the human race
I'm everywhere, everyplace . . . All I see is disgrace
I sent myself to the planet once, but that didn't work
I got murdered, but next time it's the end of the earth.
In my perfect world, Tupac and Biggie would've never died
They would be on the same team, keeping real rap alive
All eyes on them, their lyrics still hypnotize
Sky's the limit, thugs for life, until the end of time.
In my perfect world, I'd kill three birds with one stone
Instead of walking, pigs would fly home.
It's a blizzard in hell, the first time is the charm
To find peace . . . won't cost you legs and arms.
In my perfect world, I'm a 60 foot shark
A Megalodon, eating whales in the dark
I crunch down and make bones become broken
I swim around ferocious, I have no emotion.
In my perfect world, there would be a world we don't know
No heat, no cold, no rain, no snow
It's nowhere on the map, NASA can't find it
I just want to live with the one who designed it
. . . in my perfect world.

In my perfect world, there's no foster homes
All kids got both their parents, sitting high on the throne
Wouldn't have to worry about abuse or feeling neglected
Your moms and pops are there, to always keep you protected.
In my perfect world, it'll never be another nightmare
I can sleep peacefully and be in divine care
No more bad dreams, or waking up in a panic
Cold sweats is tragic, maybe its black magic?
In my perfect world, I can go back in the past
And tell myself to focus more on getting cold hard cash
Get a slow temper, play baseball in high school
. . . I'm at the top of the food chain in my school.
In my perfect world, I'd have a perfect memory
And tell you what happened centuries, before the first century
Photographic, inside I'm fantastic
Everything I see, is a certified classic
. . . in my perfect world.

In my perfect world, I'm the Hulk and Wolverine
Which means . . . I'm a killing machine, a green Christine
Chaos a routine, take your spleen
What I have in my DNA, its no vaccine.
In my perfect world, I'm getting rid of a lot of people
Who don't deserve to live in my world, where it's peaceful
111 souls is all I'm going to keep
The rest of you are gone forever under the deep.
In my perfect world, I'd never have another argument
Bone to pick, or any type of disagreement
No bickering, blow-ups, melees, squabbling
Or you walking away with a limp . . . hobbling.
In my perfect world, I wouldn't have any sin . . . I'm sinless
Wouldn't even have to ask the LORD for forgiveness
Not one unclean thought, I'm pure and perfect
Innocent, uncorrupted . . . immaculate for certain.
In my perfect world, I'm faster than the speed of light
So I go into the future to make my past and present right
I know what's gonna happen, long before it ever happens
I time travel and see what you can't imagine
. . . in my perfect world.

In my perfect world, I can use 1,000% of my brain
And literally force your life down the drain
I'll guillotine you, from a whole other continent.
No one has more confidence, or common sense.
In my perfect world, I'd never cry another tear
I wouldn't have to, sadness is disappeared
Never to return with the gloom and doom
Alone in a dark room, like a mummy tomb.
In my perfect world, I can smoke a joint and stay high for weeks
I get to live life outer space on a beach
Northern lights, amnesia, and so many others
Thanks to blue berry haze, I'm smart enough to hear colors.
In my perfect world, it's no disappointments
You can never even try to let me down . . . it's pointless.
No setbacks, failures or hurt with emotion
Or being devastated, because my heart was broken.
In my perfect world, we wouldn't need the sun to shine
Everyone would give off light, that comes from inside
Radiate, illuminate, and glow like the last dragon
I'm the master with everlasting passion
. . . in my perfect world.

In my perfect world, the only music heard is from Holy Angels
Vocals penetrating your brain from every angle
Angelic, all performances . . . authentic
The sound alone puts you to sleep, like an anesthetic.
In my perfect world, there wouldn't be fear
So everything people afraid of would never appear
Cease to have meaning, it's all going to hit the road.
Now you have absolute power and feel invincible
In my perfect world, there wouldn't be air to breathe.
I know its hard to understand, but even harder to believe
What we won't need, in this dimension.
It goes beyond all human comprehension
In my perfect world, I would have 100 sons
And each son would have 100 sons . . . we won
Never to lose, I have top shelf genetic codes
My blood carries the best strain of chromosomes.
In my perfect world, I would possess immortality
To live in a place that's of no known reality
No brutality, insanity, or fatality
Profanity, assault and battery, or tragedy
. . . in my perfect world.

In my perfect world, the Vietnam war would've never happened.
My father wouldn't have been behind enemy lines to get captured.
7.62 millimeter, pointed at his dome
And by the skin of his teeth, he made it home.
In my perfect world, c-h-i-c-a-g-o
Definitely wouldn't be a murder ca-pi-tal
Little kids could ride their bikes and play outside
Never have to worry about homicide . . . I'm alive.
In my perfect world, all ghettos would be no more
Ill-fated, stone broke, poverty-stricken and poor
. . . nobody wants to come to these neck of the woods.
I'm misunderstood, because I live in a certain neighborhood?
In my perfect world, everybody I ever hurt,
Would accept my apology.
I blame my human anatomy and physiology
Psychologically . . . I'm filled with remorse
The hatchet is buried, my life goes forth.
In my perfect world, my daughter's world would be perfect
She would always have me, and I'm something you can't purchase.
We would stay on vacation, taking trip after trip
She has anything and everything at her fingertips
. . . in my perfect world.

In my perfect world, I have Michael and Magic
Barkley, Shaq, and Wilt . . . and we letting teams have it
Kobe and Ivo . . . Bird, KG and the captain Kareem
You have 0, we scored 203.
In my perfect world, I have Montana to Rice
Moss, Irvin, Beckam Jr, so my receivers are tight.
Bo and Sweetness running the ball, Tony Gonzalez at the end.
With the '85 Bear's defense, we always win!
In my perfect world, I can speak any language in existence
. . . this universe or another solar system
I can give and take information
Have a conversation, about the creation of the constellations.
In my perfect world, nine eleven is just another day
Instead of being a memorial of people who died a horrific way
Over 3,000 dead, that could still be breathing
But Al Qaeda and America, left families forever grieving
In my perfect world, it's only one race
You don't have to worry about what you look like,
Nobody has a face
No such thing as a master race, not in this place
You don't ever have to be concerned about the weight . . . say grace
. . . in my perfect world.

In my perfect world, it wouldn't be a conspiracy
To depopulate my people, but you're not listening or hearing me.
They give us military guns plus kilos of drugs to use
Which equals an explosion, because they lit the fuse.
In my perfect world, the voices in my head pay rent
Because for them to stay here, is about dollars and cents
I can deal with the noise and the ones who are sadistic
But I can't deal with disrespect, those getting evicted.
In my perfect world, demons wouldn't follow me anymore.
They forget all about me and wouldn't see me anymore
They couldn't show me temptations, entrap or entice me
Sweeting up a situation and lure me in precisely.
In my perfect world, I'm happy and smile everyday
So no matter how hard somebody try, it can't be taken away.
I hold on to my good spirits, like a anaconda squeezing you.
Never losing my peace of mind, I'm always keeping you.
In my perfect world, I have the power of 50 Mike Tysons.
When I punch you, your head blows up like a bomb from Isis
The opposite of niceness, here comes the crisis
1 uppercut and you're knocked out lifeless
. . . in my perfect world.

In my perfect world, the devil would finally leave me alone
Never again would I hear him say, "I'm coming for your soul"
Or constantly telling me, "I want you dead or in jail . . .
so you can waste away the rest of your pathetic life in a cell."
In my perfect world, it's impossible for me to feel depressed
Down and out, suicidal, sad, hopelessness
Spiritless, mentally defeated and lost.
The power I posses inside, somehow has been turned off.
In my perfect world, I can never make a mistake
Like getting kicked out of college, or having nowhere to escape.
Held back by females, I should have been let go.
Keeping misery around, just means you can't grow.
In my perfect world, I'm resurrecting a chosen few from the grave
Breathe new life into their lungs, return to the stage
Celebration, you're back to civilization
Rose from your sleep and finally re-awakened.
In my perfect world, I'd know everything
The meaning of life and my purpose, as a super-human being
Before the past, no month, no time, no year
After the future, I've already seen crystal clear
. . . in my perfect world.

In my perfect world, the devil would stop trying to kill me
Drive my truck off the bridge, thoughts are eerie
Shoot myself in the heart so my brain can be studied.
My room looks like a horror flick . . . everywhere is bloody
The ceiling, the walls, I'm getting phone calls
Saying, "you're worthless, because of you're flaws, you're an oddball
Overall . . . you're destined to fall."
I hang up, because they lies, I'm above all
In my perfect world, satan would stop hating
And congratulate me, for trying so hard to make it
. . . Never giving up, despite what I had to go through.
He gave me a hug and said he felt he was supposed to
. . . bought me every pair of black Jordans
And apologized for telling me, you should've been aborted.
Even offered me remorse, compassion, and kindness
And said, "we can put all the bad of the past behind us."
In my perfect world, the evil one would turn and stay good
Become loving and respectful, without being misunderstood
Instead of the father of lies, he's the father of the truth
Dedicated and devoted to protection of the youth
. . . in my perfect world.

In my perfect world, all my organs are re-born
So anything that deteriorated over time, it's all gone
Brand new, unused like it's still in the package
My heart, lungs, liver, and brain . . . have no damage.
In my perfect world, I would have the perfect wife
Her main goal is to make sure, that I have a perfect life
She everything I could ever have, want or need
I got what I asked for, as I live and breathe.
In my perfect world, I could teleport to Paris
Italy and Rome, my talent I inherit and
Make sure I see every wonder of the world twice
My eyes delight from the sight . . . a GOD given right.
In my perfect world, I would never get angry.
If I blow my top, then you would have to restrain me
But it's not me, it's the demon that lives deep within.
My inner abyss, my levi a thin
In my perfect world, I'm Sampson and Goliath
A 10 foot, super strong, all-powerful giant
With my bare hands, I'll break your bones like potato chips
It's on to the next life for you, have a safe trip
. . . in my perfect world.

In my perfect world, I'm a 2,000 lb. gorilla, werewolf, grizzly bear
In the blink of an eye, I'll kill you anywhere
Anytime . . . you're not yours, but mine
I waste nothing, I eat the meat off your spine.
In my perfect world, my faith can make anything move
Feel yourself rise off the ground, right now as I'm talking to you
I believe so hard, I don't have to assume
Because eventually, the worse situation will improve.
In my perfect world, I breathe fire and spit alien blood
Melt your flesh, cremate all your love
It won't be anyone left when I'm done
No ashes, my words burn hotter than the sun.
In my perfect world, I can fight like Bruce Lee
Disconnect your neck, it's none like me
Injuries I give to you are untreatable
I'm undefeated, the very best . . . unbeatable.
In my perfect world, I was given a sacred ancient book
Called "The Secret Secrets of Women"
So of course I took a look
I was told, there's only a certain few that I can reveal
Be romantic and listen, the love will stay real
. . . in my perfect world.

In my perfect world, all my prayers get answered
And that's why to this very day, I'm still handsome.
All my requests, begging a billion times saying please
Paid off, no more 2 and 3 hours on my knees.
In my perfect world, GOD gave me the power,
To send whoever I want to hell.
Everlasting punishment is where you live . . . oh well
I'm never bringing you back, I did what I should
You had plenty of chances, now you're gone for good.
In my perfect world, it's only one GOD to worship
So if you're atheist, the Father is your new purpose.
No Allah, no Budda, Catholics or Hindu
Scientology, Jehovahs Witnesses or Jews.
In my perfect world, God removes all evil
People who're deceitful, douse with ten gallons of diesel
And light a match, burn all the weasels
Incinerate your soul, AWOL . . . no retrieval.
In my perfect world, the LORD is back right here in the flesh
I'm a witness, of being blessed by the best of the best
The Holy City will be shown, not to be overlooked
You can't get in, unless your name is written in The BOOK
. . . in my perfect world.

Not For Sale
By Marvin O'Neal

A Total Waste

Wasted Time, Wasted Dreams
Wasted Opportunities, Wasted Jobs
Wasted Money, Wasted Women
Wasted School, Wasted Cars
Wasted Love, Wasted Energy
Wasted Brain Cells, Wasted Workouts
Wasted Chances, Wasted Thoughts
Wasted Situations, Wasted Talent
Wasted Knowledge, Wasted Wisdom
Wasted Gas, Wasted Prayers
Wasted Tears, Wasted Beers
Wasted Years, Wasted Decades
Wasted Blood, Wasted Sleep
Wasted Food, Wasted Happiness
Wasted Sacrifices, Wasted Friendships
Wasted Nights, Wasted Days
Wasted Anger, Wasted Hatred
Wasted Feelings, Wasted Reality
Wasted Breath, Wasted Health
Wasted Existence, Wasted Intelligence
. . . A Total Waste of Life

This Dimension

The devil is my immortal enemy
It's a war for my soul and he's not stealin it from me
I fight with all the might I can possibly bring
With the strength of every king, my GOD is Everything
My confession, I keep nuclear weapons
Once I push the button, it's no protection
Teach life a lesson, death I'm destined
But not before the Lord come back, HE takin me to heaven
A world of 7 deadly sins
It starts from the end, then begins
There is no middle, no grey area
I heard the sounds of hell . . . it's nothing scarier
The earth is doomed, fate has a mission
1 of the biggest problems, people don't listen
Niggaz especially, homicide daily
All I can do is my best and work with what HE gave me
The moon sets and the sun rises
The words I speak, severely paralyses
Suicide is . . . not a decision
2094 is my vision, keep living

Taking Back What's Mine

Time to take my life back
Take my time back, take my health back
Take back my money, take back my career
Take my mind and brain back, take my soul back
Take back my supreme confidence and what I'm owed back
Take my body back, heart and lungs back
Take my respect back, my intellect back
Take my POWER back, take my strength back
Take my talent back, take my credit back
Take my territory back, take my family back
Take my happiness back, so I can smile back
Take my writing, readin and believin back
Take my purpose and why I'm here back
Take my passion and drive back . . . I need that
Take my past back, take my future where I need it to go
Take my present and make the most of my gifts
Take my shine back, take EVERYTHING that's mine back
Take my decisions and mistakes back
Take my dreams back, going full head of steam back
My mean is back, tyrannical animal
Full moon werewolf, flesh eating cannibal
. . . forever I'm back

I Can't Thank You Enough

I thank you LORD, for my countless blessings
Teachin me lessons and forgiving me of a billion confessions
You gave me hard tough love and discipline
You definitely got my attention, for all the times I wasn't listening
I was given a gift of a daughter, who stands next to you
Without her . . . I wouldn't even know what to do
I wouldn't even have a clue, my life would be worthless
Erase me from existence, my life would be birthless
You saved my soul from eternal torture
I'm going to stay on the right path and receive my fortune
I fight against the devil and demons daily
I kick them out my head, but they come back . . . it's krazy
It's hard to hit something that's an unseen spirit
So I use mental machine guns and keep shooting until I kill it
Joy comes in the morning, bad news without warning
Good vs. evil, the war never gets boring
I'm the re-birth, re-cycled, regenerated version
Trained by the best of the best, but I still keep learning
I'm lucky and fortunate to be smiling
I took my life back and now the money piling
. . . I cant thank you enough

Sworn Enemies Part 1

Before I was even conceived, I was already hated
Despised, detested and disliked by satan
Demons set traps, pitfalls and mishaps
Play your life like a game of craps, til it collapse
Or cave in, I'm so far way in
I can't blame men, but the evil that lives within
Sick with sin, sad to say . . . it'll never end
Let me live again when I was 10, divided by 10
It's no GOD without the devil, no treats just trickery
No mystery, the proof is in the history
War, disease and famine
Hell is a real place, worse than anything you
could ever possibly imagine
The mind can't fathom, feel heat from the devils mouth
Whenever it's open . . . something wicked is coming out
Burn baby burn, he the most heartless, sharpest, smartest
Type to eat a rotten carcass, prince of darkness
He strangles your prayers, as they float in the air
You think they going to the LORD? It's not getting there
Unfair, he doesn't play by rules
He just wants to see you achieve your end and lose
. . . Your whole soul in the process

Sworn Enemies Part 2

I feel like I'm trapped in a bottomless pit, always falling
I can't escape the darkness, it's always calling
Demons follow me, then they walk away
This happens every day, I rebuke them just to get them away
Why me is the question, I've been thru enough
It's a warfare of the spirits, in my GOD I trust
Demonic, what I fight against is diabolic
Tempted by the demoness, because she's erotic
Exotic, you might not understand my logic
She over the edge psychotic . . . trying to get your wallet
Devilism is all day terrorism
They quick to give you ignorance, instead of wisdom
Feed you foolishness, abusiveness
Destruction of your own soul, ruthlessness
Slit your wrist in a hot bath, breathe poisonous gas
Live slow but die fast, a wicked plan
Protect your soul, the onslaught has begun
No heat or light from the sun . . . life is done
Can't run, can't hide, from the battleground warzone
Cyanide suicide, you on your own

I Promise Part 1

As long as I have breath to breathe . . .
I promise to keep my promise
Live up to and keep my foundation solid
Can't lie to myelf, so I must be honest
I'm a god, so I want me a goddess
I promise to never abuse or mistreat
Never cheat, I'll cook you something good to eat
Wash your feet, it's a marathon not a track meet
Having you in my life, makes mine complete
I promise to always be a real father
Because of my child I'm calmer and do things in her honor
Everyday I'm stronger, pure as holy water
It's nothing I wouldn't give or do for my daughter
I promise to always keep my faith
No matter what adversity, decides to get in my face
Invade my space, or shift into whatever kind of shape
My fulfillment to be resilient . . . remain great

I Promise Part 2

As long as I have breath to breathe . . .
I promise to my best friend and brother on death row
To keep letters and money coming, even though the mail slow
Stay visiting, so I can see the face and smile that I know
You right here in my heart and I'm never letting go
I promise on my soul, to reach all my goals
Grab hold, take control and get out this hell hole
Mayweather money, I got duffel bags full of bank rolls
Whenever in the street, I'm safe because a tank goes
I promise to continue to live and live smarter
Y'all go hard, but I'm forced to go harder
Protected by GOD'S armor, HE my bodyguard
For HIM, I'll sacrifice both my arms
I promise, I'll a be the one to get the last laugh
Cut you in 1/2, the whole scene is a blood bath
Feed you to the cats and the rats, but instead of getting mad
I think and plan out ways to spend cash

Since I'm a Cop

Since I'm a cop and you don't look like me, you getting shot
In the middle of your forehead is a big red dot
Since I'm a cop, you face down on the floor
With my knee in your back, right in front of the liquor store
Since I'm a cop, I'm the happiest man alive
I got a license to kill, so a plan I devised
. . . here take your phone, group text your last goodbyes
Paramedics tried, but they couldn't revive . . . I'm taking lives
Since I'm a cop, I'm ruining your whole night
Pull you over, harass you, and violate the body of your wife
Since I'm a cop, I'm disregarding your civil rights
And beat you worse than the Passion of the Christ
Since I'm a cop, I'm purposely targeting Europeans
So they can feel what it's like to be treated less than a human being
. . . you think your skin color makes you better?
I'm ready to annihilate your kind and get rid of yall forever
Since I'm a cop, you paying me four g's a month
Like the mafia or you taking a ride in my trunk
Since I'm a cop, I'm a make sure the jury convicts
So you spend decades behind bars for a crime you didn't commit
Since I'm a cop, I'm acquitted of all murder charges
Because the judge wasn't convinced . . . case dismissed

Money Mayweather

2/24/77
I was born with gifts that God Himself gave me from heaven
Grew up in oppression, highly aggressive
I learned how to box and turned my hands into deadly weapons
A maniac in the ring, fight me at your own discretion
I became 50-0, so I'm never second
Hall of Fame? No question . . . 15 titles
5 different weight classes, beat all my rivals
Pound for pound, round for round, made them all look like clowns
I hit you so hard, you lose your sight and sound
On my head is a crown, supreme king of the ring
I've made so much money, I can buy anything
Fill my pool with cash and swim in it
My house so big a 1,000 people can live in it
Living my dream everyday in the real world
I do hard work, for my sons and baby girls

Unvisible

Where did I come from? Where am I going?
I can't be stopped, limited or blocked . . . I'm free flowing
Never held back or held down, I'm all around
Everywhere I go . . . I surround
It could be the playground, or a small town
A big city downtown, your town, Georgetown
Whenever I feel pressure I move
I can't be hugged, especially in a bad mood
I change quickly, from 1 direction to the next
Like Bill Bixby, turn into something you respect
I'm strong enough to pull trees from the roots
Separate your house from the roof . . . documented proof
I help lions smell prey from a mile away
The talent I possess, you cannot outweigh
I just play, the only cards I was dealt
On earth, in outer space . . . I'm always felt

Birthrights

Life, liberty and the pursuit of happiness
But all I see on this land is the total opposite
Death, slavery and the pursuit of nothingness
Production of destruction, made people lovingless
So because of this, I'm respectless to your stars and stripes
Not go change who I am, I'm a live my life
I never asked to be hated and stereotyped
So I conceal and carry all day and all night
My undeniable right, to do whatever I like
But I'm judged by the color of my skin over insight
U.S.A you can burn, along with your pledge
the constitution is on fire, as I speak revenge
these states was built on liars, assassins and murderers
rapists, who whole intent was to murder us
I'm not a dog I'm a god, made in His eyes
Born wise . . . my soul is immortalized

It Rains Diamonds

Morning, night, winter, spring
My power creates power for me to do anything
I smell shapes and touch every emotion
My inner drive is alive, a tidal wave from the ocean
I taste words, delicious verbs on my tongue
Eat til I'm full, clean my plate . . . not a crumb
Turn my dreams into movie scenes, which can be seen
400 ft. screens, I'm filled with dopamine
I took a trip to the other side of the moon
and saw things you would never believe was actually true
I kiss lightning and make babies with thunder
I'm unique when I speak, just like a prime number
Golden skies, fresh cut red grass
Streets of precious gems, the future is the past

Three Greenlights

My **fire** is lit, with a will to achieve
In myself I believe . . . undeceived

My **passion** is a sea of flames burning ablaze
Red hot to the touch, like heat from sun rays

My **drive** inside, intensifies and becomes greater
Than it was yesterday . . . I'm a terminator

My **discipline** is grizzly strong, self-mastery
Control destiny with the master key

My **perseverance** has endurance of a permanent marathon
Endure the pain, re-focus and carry on

My **confidence**, is super supremacy
Nothing in my chemistry, has any misery

My **responsibility**, never give up or quit
Nuts and guts on the table, with a perfect spirit

My **purpose**, is to get there and live in a dream
Success everywhere, counting money a routine

Colorless

If it wasn't for color, I wouldn't be judged
Or looked at as a criminal or a menacing thug
Drug dealer, gangbanger, rapist and burglarer
Not guilty like O.J. but I'm still a murderer
Black eyed peas, collard greens, the cornbread thickens
A hot bowl of chitterlings, watermelon or foods high in fat
Pork rinds, bar BBQ, hot chips I'm buying that
If it wasn't for color, I wouldn't be illiterate
Uneducated, a dumb retarded stupid idiot
With the I.Q. of a monkey, chimpanzee or baboon
I can't be a tycoon, just a dirty raccoon
If it wasn't for color, it wouldn't be strange
for me to play hockey
Golf and baseball or be a horse jockey
But I'm seen with tattoos and a basketball
Even though I possess the talent to master it all
If it wasn't for color, all the women wouldn't have attitudes
Or be angry all the time, waking up in a bad mood
Public-aid, medi-cade, getting pregnant for a check
Who's your baby daddy? The Maury show had to background check
If it wasn't for color, you would know we was here 1st
It was 1 continent, which is why we everywhere on the earth
It's a fact I'm not black, because my blood is pure
Don't worry about color, is the solution and cure

Complete Happiness

Happiness is something that cannot be bought
Even with the best trackers, it cannot be caught
It will literally elude you and disappear from your sight
If you ever see it again, you better hold on for dear life
With all your might, grip extra tight
No matter what, never let go . . . darkness becomes light
I shine so bright you need shades just to look at me
I'm taking back everything that was ever took from me
Or taken . . . this the resurrected re-awaken
It's in the core of my bones, everyday is a celebration
Happiness is something that makes me cry
But my tears have smiley faces, joy is why
It's a feeling of euphoria, so glorious
I'm a real warrior . . . VICTORIOUS

Are You a Goddess

You're a sight for sore eyes, I think about your face and eyes
and realize anytime, I can taste what's mine
Because your skin smooth like a new born baby
I'm so attracted I could look at you daily
Real hair, real nails, real body, real lashes
Your beauty surpasses, far above the average
Are you a goddess? Do you know how to communicate?
Can I trust you with my life? My love illuminates
Radiates and beams like the sunlight . . . moonlight
My thirst for you goes to new heights
Are you a goddess? Do you hunger for me?
How big is you appetite or voracity?
Do you yearn to kiss me or smell my scent?
How bad do you miss me, from time we spent?
Are you a goddess? Crave and desire me
Admire me, the way you are inspires me
and requires me, to give you everything I can possibly give
Happy and healthy is how we can live . . . I'm positive

Impacted Influences

Tupac, Scarface, KRS-1
Ice Cube, Raekwon, Biggie and Big Pun
Kool G Rap, Red Man, 8-Ball
and MJG, Method Man, Above the Law
Chuck D, IMD, Common and Game
Bone Thugs, E-40, Big Daddy Kane
The Lady of Rage, Black Thought, AMG
TLC, Twista, Outcast and Jay-Z
Master P, Snoop D-O-double G
Afrika Bambatta, Luda and 50
D-R-E, Future, Daz and Kurupt
Hammer, The Lox, Nas, Can-I-Bus
Lauryn Hill, MC Lyte, The Brat, E-V-E
Lil Kim, Bahamadia and Foxy
Missy, Mia X, D.O.C
LL, Big L, Treach, Ice-T
Warren G, Heavy D, Run D.M.C
M&M, Cam'ron, Juve, Kool Moe D
Easy E, MC Ren, MC 8
3-6 Mafia, Cypress Hill, UGK
Rakim, The WU, Nate Dogg and Slick Rick
Tribe Called Quest, Goodie Mob, DJ Quik
Gravediggaz, Too Short, Bushwick, Biz Markie
Gang Starr, Fat Joe, T.I., Willie D
Dmx, Busta, Jeru and Jeezy
Pete Rock and CL Smooth, EPMD

Misery Hates My Company

Your miserable, mad, depressed and sad
Jealous, lonely, insecure and phony
And you not bringing me down . . . no way no how
Your empty inside, an annoyance, joyless
Suicidal, dreary, dead done and weary
And you not bringing me down . . . no way no how
Your whole life is morbid, discouraging, distorted
You stay unhappy and negative, pessimistic, uncompetitive
And you not bringing me down . . . no way no how
You feel unwanted, unattractive, useless, inactive
Counterproductive, distracted, abandoned, impactless
Helpless, non-adaptive
A prisoner of yourself, your own soul is held captive
And you not bringing me down . . . no way no how

Half of the Whole Part 1

Everything about you is love, my heart can fill with hate
You always on time and I'm late . . . we both give and take
I'll pour down like rain, you're different like a snowflake
I'm patient, but when it comes to seeing you . . . I can't wait
I'm cruel inhumane, your pleasure I'm pain
Supersmart is what you are, when sometimes I have no brain
I glow like the moon, you shine like the sun
It feel like I always lose, but having you . . . I won
We're so much alike, but so very different
I'm insignificant and you're so magnificent
It's all or nothing, either we in or out
I have total faith and you have no doubt
From dawn til dust, it's them against us
I'm ready for war, having peace is a must
You create I'll destroy, curse and bless
I used to be the worse, but now that your mine . . . I'm the best
Follow my lead, where your weak I'm strong
I can't turn it off, my tenaciousness stays on
I'll live and die for you, laugh and cry with you
Don't ask why . . . the earth and sky is you

Half of the Whole Part 2

Be for I met you. . . all I ever seen was the dark,
now I just see the light
After you came into my life, we talking husband and wife
I feel fantastic day and night, whatever I throw you catch
Even if I say no, you persuade me to say yes
We more private than public, positive than negative
All we want to do is become chief executives
and live the rich life, forget all about being poor
We never settling for less, we always want more
Bank accounts and pocketbooks not skinny but extra fat
I got your front and your back, I'll protect and attack
While most couples stay horizontal, we going vertical
GOD gave you all to me . . . because he's merciful
I couldn't treat you ordinary, you way to special
We don't argue but agree to fulfill potential
Conversation . . . essential like sugar and salt
Right and left, up and down, true and false
From the coldest winter, to the hottest summer
I'll go through hell, if your heaven I discover
I'm a travel east to west, then north and south
Your the beginning and end, I can't live without

Half of the Whole Part 3

I'm so cold I burn and melt you like butter
Everybody else can freeze, I wants for no other
We'll start with breakfast and finish with dinner
You not a loser but a winner, too sweet to be bitter
We professionals masters, passed a beginner
I try to live like a saint, pray for me . . . I'm a sinner
Not my opinion but a fact
All the money in the world isn't enough, I love you more than that
When I rise you rise, when I fall you still rise
You the most intriguing being I've ever seen . . . dead or alive
I'll add and multiply all the good, subtract and divide all the bad
I can't let you go, you're the best thing I've ever had
My heart is open just for you, but closed to the majority
Your not on the back burner, but a main priority
Superiority and power . . . happens normally
It's not strange to me, that I feel for you enormously
I hunger for you, I thirst for you
2nd doesn't, exist, I'm 1st for you
A GOD and a GODDESS, trying to get all the knowledge
We flow like liquids . . . titanium solid

Half of the Whole Part 4

I'm happy and healthy when you're here,
sad and sick when you're away
I want you near not far . . . I need you everyday
You give me hope when I'm hopeless
and help me re-focus, whenever I get distracted somehow you notice
And tell me I'm somebody, when I feel like a nobody
I get hugs so tight, you warm my whole body
I'm coke you pepsi, 7up and Im sprite
You a bird rising early, I'm a owl at night
His and hers Lamborghinis, we finally multi-millionaires
You have a heiress to the throne, I have my sole heir
You talk and I'll listen . . . any question I'll answer
I care about nothing in life, you all that matters
Fall, spring, disguise, discover
No female has ever loved me more . . . except my mother
My sister and my daughter
Touch 1 hair on any of their head and meet my horror
You support not discourage and want my talent to flourish
You always feed me and keep me well nourished
Finding you was like finding bars of gold
For you not to see death . . . I'll give up my soul

Daddy's Baby

I loved you be for you had any shape or form
I loved you be for you was ever even born . . . and be for that day
I never knew what being a father was really like
Until I saw you and got light from your life
Never have I seen anything more beautiful
The love I have for you is indisputable
We share a bond that goes beyond l-o-v-e
The only thing above you and me is G-O-D
My devotion and dedication gives me appreciation
You saved my life, from the beginning of you creation
It's no number big enough to describe your worth
Not even all the money on the entire planet earth
The universe is cheap, compared to your pricelessness
Nothing in existence has more righteousness
I love you for all of eternity
Forever and Evermore . . . ETERNALLY

Medicine Volume 1
The Above Space Edition

Medicine Part 1

Let me diagnose, care, treat and prevent
I'm a get you back to normal 100%
You can smoke me, snort me, drink me, inject me
Swallow me like a pill . . . heal you effectively
Relieve your pain, take away your migraine
No more schizophrenia, I'll keep you sane
Inhale me and breathe me deep into your mind
Overqualified to change anything I find
Revitalize, rejuvenate, remember, re-educate
Overdose on me, no need to resuscitate
Absorb my remedy, as I soak into your skin
I'm better than any narcotic or hallucinogen
Heroine and morphine wears off, I don't
They'll destroy and kill you, I never will and wont
But take you to the 10th dimension, with one prescription
Listening and reading my words the addiction

Medicine Part 2

I'll hit you harder than a poor man's ecstasy
Trazadone, Adderall . . . I'm your destiny
A necessity, because I successfully
Make you better every day . . . that's my specialty
I'm above all moon rocks, Zoloft and nose candy
Fifth's of the world's best cognac and brandy
Even if the angels in heaven gave you dust
It still wouldn't be more than me or enough
I won't make your teeth rotten like oxycotin
Or make you kill yourself, because you convinced
you under the bottom
Methadone, Vicodin can't help you win
Even when the pain leaves, it returns again
. . . now you looking down the wrong end of the telescope
My words are purer than dope . . . the antidote
Hope and healing, talented enough to save all
You'll never be depressed again or ever fall
I'm a trained, unchained, master of all masters
Repeat my speech, study every chapter
and watch your life improve, enhance, enrich
Enlighten and slowly become perfect

Medicine Part 3

I can take you so high, you looking down on space
My literature literally takes you to the right place
All you have to do is take time to listen
I'm your new physician, here to cure your condition
Zanex, crystal meth, mushrooms made of magic
Still got you stuck in the attic . . . post traumatic
Problematic, you wasted all your talent
But one of my doses brings you back . . . automatic
Decades of abuse won't even matter
Instantly gives you life, from zombie and cadaver
Two poems twice a day, cleans out your bloodstream
Circulating thru your system . . . self-esteem
Self-respect, self-righteousness
Self-control, now you full of confidence
Eat my words like a chewable tablet
Stick em on your arm like patches . . . make it happen

Money is No Good Here Part 1

I'm free like my heart beating pumping blood
2 miles an hour through my veins pumping love
I'm free like hugs and kisses, give and receive
I need them every day, the feeling helps me breathe
Mentally, spiritually, I'm permanently free
My personality was a gift given to me
I'm free like a parolee, wrongfully accused and convicted
The day came . . . I got my golden ticket
I'm so free, I'm a tree that'll never get cut down
Forever bloom and blossom, roots stay in the ground
I'm free like a giant tsunami wave, atomic bomb power
Anything, anyone in my way . . . devoured
I'm free like a slave, who finally escaped
Now I work for myself and the feeling is great
I'm free like the wind blowing, so cool on my face
I can go anywhere, anytime, anyplace

Money is No Good Here Part 2

I'm free like the sun, watch me rise and set
My inside is a full moon, give light to darkness
A park bench, I can sit on and pay no price
Meditate on my life . . . trips to paradise
I'm free like imagination, mine has no bounds
My knowledge, wisdom, and understanding is profound
I'm free like music, I listen surround sound
No choice but to use it . . . takes me above the clouds
I'm free like prayers I want GOD to hear and answer
Fix all my disasters, LORD and MASTER
I'm free like memories that make me smile
Especially the ones that make me proud . . . I laugh out loud
I'm free like the words I write down and speak
Dates and time have no fee . . . 7 days in a week
I'm free like salvation, it was already paid
All I had to do was ask and my soul was saved

Impacted Influences Part 2

Mary J. Blidge, Chanel Live, Tone Loc and Shyne
Grandmaster Flash and The Furious 5
Alicia Keys, Aaliyah, Digable Planets
MC Breed, Gang Starr, Boogie Monsters, Janet
Black Moon, Salt and Pepa, Das Efx
Brand Nubian, The Pharcyde, Alchemist
Beastie Boys, Fat Boys, Michael Jackson, Chubb Rock
Mos Def, Lil John, Swizzy, Pharoah Monch
Whodini, Trick Daddy, MC Shan
Capone-N-Noreaga, Trina, X-Clan
Beanie Seagal, Do or Die, Krucial Conflict
Public Enemy, Arrested Development
Vanilla Ice, Ultra Magnetic MC's
Kurtis Blow, Naughty by Nature, The Fugees
Kris Kross, Killa Priest, Treacheous 3
Hieroglyphics, Young MC, BDP
Souls of Mischief, The Roots, 2 Live Crew
Lords of the Underground, 3rd Base, Ja Rule
Jungle Brothers, De La Soul, Sugar Hill Gang
Stetsasonic, Doug E Fresh, House of Pain
Sista Souljah, Gangsta Boo, Rah Digga, Nikki D
JJ Fad, Queen Latifa, Heather B
Monie Love, YO-YO, Boss and Brandy
En Vogue, Xscape, Apllonia, Vanity
Sir Mix-a-lot, Mac 10, Master Ace
Outlaws, Digitial Underground, Rob Base

The God of Evil

1st beast of the revelation, masquerader of light
The morning star, anti-Christ, anti-life
Destruction, delusionary, scary, destroyer
Ruler of demons, on a mission coming for you
King of hell, wicked thief in the night
Warlord of the bottomless pit, never polite
Sinister . . . with a goal to keep you prisoner
No longer a visitor, hell bound with a signature
Father of lies, diabolical diabolos
Disintegrate all hopes, knife at your own throat
Darkness has a prince, your viewed as worthless
A rat snake, with a steal, kill, ill purpose
A Venus hot furnace, a realm of torturous heat
Once you in, no way to get out . . . you dog meat
The great dragon, dishonest, deceptive, deceitful
god of this world, source of all evil

Your Not Wife Material Part 1

Rain, hail, sleet, snow
The seasons change, but a hoe is always go be a hoe
You can take the pig out the slop, but eventually
they go back to the slop
It's in their nature, like donuts to a cop
You're a bimbo, slore, wanch to the core
Your life is a perfect and complete failure
So damaged, it's no way to restore
Unrepairable, what are you even living for?
You could never or ever be somebodies wife
Your the worse half, cheating on your wedding night
How could somebody ever trust you, the jig is up
Your infected with bad luck, crooked and corrupt
The life of a mistress, the best you'll be
You dead in my eyes, so blessed be
You're a floozy, harlot, tramp of the street
A scam artist, defrauder, straight piece of meat
Any man take your hand in marriage and matrimony
Better be prepared to pay cash for alimony
Females like you deserve to get the boot
Burn in hell . . . the mother of prostitutes

Your Not Wife Material Part 2

You don't believe what I believe, you don't cook, you don't clean
You not trust worthy, an adulterous queen
It's all about being selfless, but you selfish
You supposed to have my back and be helpful . . . you helpless
Dishonest, disloyal, your insides are all spoiled
Disrespectful and your plans are foiled
Unappreciative and you don't listen
Instead of being my soul mate, your enemy opposition
My premonition tells me nothing but suspicion
Any guy you get with, becomes a demolition
A heart condition, his life was not worth living
Because of how you treated him . . . ungiving
Your compatible with none, communication sucks
What's your #1 priority? You not us
The sight of you makes me vomit, you not respected
You're an abomination and respectless

Your Not Wife Material Part 3

You're a home wrecker and possess no wisdom
Unprepared for the future, you have no vision
No understanding, no knowledge to keep a home happy
It's like you was born in garbage . . . trashy and nasty
Without honor, your spirit has no worth
When it comes to a wretched person, I think of you 1st
Your life is beyond cursed, pitiful and shameful
You somebody I could put my hands on and strangle
Tear you to pieces mangle, from 90 degree angles
I'm a make sure whatever you feel is painful
Gentle and quiet? Nope you loud and defiant
Non-compliant, late night lying with a client
Have a baby by you? Why? Your womb is polluted
Hazardous to my health, I'll let them do it
I wish you was dead and every chick just like you
Cease to exist, nobody will wife you

Your Not Wife Material Part 4

Just because you're a female doesn't mean you deserve a baby
Your certified krazy, who is not a lady
A soul mate, housewife, or companion
Instead of giving an abundance of love . . . you gave a famine
A failure and straight neglected your man
You lied to the cops and they arrested your man
Your future husband, the groom, Mr. Right
Your love is all dark no light . . . rude, impolite
Ill-bred, ill-mannered, high hopes got shattered
Everything he tried to do for you, never even mattered
You nowhere near elegant and have no etiquette
Everyday your fiancé drinks with pink elephants
Going back and forth to court, trying to get a settlement
Thoughtless, you was born with no intelligence
No kindness, mindless and spineless
You never getting married . . . to material minded

Your Not Wife Material Part 5

I stayed overnight in a hotel, with a bad little chick
I saw you in the lobby and seen who you was with
It wasn't your husband, but your new loverboy
I'm a do you, like how they burned down Troy
No mercy, sympathy, compassion or empathy
I'm a keep you on fire . . . endlessly
All you do is bring stress, uneasiness
No progress and no success
Worry and aggravation, unfaithfulness
Anxiety, irritation . . . is what you do best
Streetwalker, sex worker, dumb broad, queen slut
Treat you like a black widow and leave you untouched
You broke every last vow that you promised
and never once did you not bring drama
Unfriendly, unloving, unbecoming
You a match made in hell, I'm a stay away from you

He Died and Made Me GOD Part 1

I twist fate and surgically strike
I talk to myself, because great minds think alike
Never say die, I'm built to never quit
I sleep on a bed of roses, to my heart's content
Whenever you see me, you see the spitting image of GOD
Me and my best friend, like 2 peas in a pod
Danger is real, but fear is a choice
Talented beyond belief . . . the trophy I hoist
When a man fears GOD, everything fears him
Only 2 things left to do . . . sink or swim
I try hard not to fail, but won't fail to try
The architect of my fortune, my impulse is blind
Strong enough to overcome the weak, I'm filled with power
Smart enough to over the strong, they run like cowards
A wise man changes, a fool stays the same
I'm at the apex of life, a whole new ball game

He Died and Made Me GOD Part 2

I'm all bite and no bark, from the end to the start
Conquer and divide, war is an art
Add fuel to my flames, get treated like dirt
If it's the last thing I do, make sure you hurt
I'm the best thing since the wheel, spokes need oil
Pressure breaks the pipes, don't let the food spoil
. . . a friend in need, is a friend indeed
Wear my heart on my sleeve, believe and receive
I made it BIG, certified, bona fide
Better late than never, blessings come in disguise
I don't gamble, so I won't risk it all
Don't have a care in the world, I'm having a ball
Living life calm like a toad in the sun
I jumped over the moon, compare me to none
Last but not least, diamonds cut diamonds
Tropical islands, perfect timing

He Died and Made Me GOD Part 3

I got my cake and I'm eating it too
With cherries on top . . . no catch 22
In my possession, is the golden key
Never had it so good, I'm blessed to be me
Drastic times call for drastic measures
So I keep my heart hidden like a priceless treasure
You a yesterday's man, it's my time for glory
I got a stash full of cash . . . my inventory
Not a dime to the dozen, I'm rare like a red moon
Blue stars, white nights, real life cartoons
I work hard like a beaver, it's my nature to build
Nothing can stop fate, destiny I fulfill
You can't move standing still, so I go the extra mile
Multiplied by, 1,000 drink my coke and I smile
The corridors of power, is where I make my decisions
On a course of collision, to live what I envision

He Died and Made Me GOD Part 4

I'm a give you a fate worse than death and rain down hell
Put your head in a box and post mark it priority mail
Throw you to the wolves, let your blood get tasted
Flesh gets ripped, now I'm off to the races
Kick the bucket, eat all the dust you bite
Whenever we cross paths . . . be prepared to fight
I just might kill you and your friend with 1 bullet
At the moment of truth, the trigger I'm pulling
My madness has a method, I'll rack your brain
Hang you out to dry . . . nothing remains
You barked up the wrong tree, a tiger came down
Between you and me, your body will never be found
Your life is dirt cheap and you don't stand a chance
I'm a proven nightmare, make you piss in your pants
The moral to the story is no silver lining
You done for, done in . . . no surviving

He Died and Made Me GOD Part 5

A fish rots from the head down, let me start at the top
I wouldn't be caught dead with you . . . like it or not
Speak of the devil, let's get down to the crunch
I got enough on my plate raincheck you on lunch
Pulled the rabbit out of the hat, took the cat out of the bag
Just because you cry doesn't mean your sad
Not go twist arms and pull teeth, I'm a cut to the chase
At 1st sight it's on, I remember your face
More than one way to skin a cat, curiosity kilt it
No point to waste tears on milk after you spilt
A drowning man holds a straw to save his life
You try to breathe under water . . . adios goodnight
Whenever you around I smell nothing but rats
That's why you get a cold shoulder, facts is facts
Waste not want not, leopards can't change their spots
Like father like daughter . . . chip off the old block

He Died and Made Me GOD Part 6

At 1st sight we clicked and had a match made connection
Heavenly is your body, I long for your affection
We see eye to eye and speak the same language
Let's go with the flow and continue to maintain it
When it rains cats and dogs, we keep each other's back
and figure out solutions to problems . . . plan the attack
You look like a million dollars and dress to kill
I'll go to the ends of the earth for you . . . pay all the bills
Work my fingers to the bone, for my family to eat
Unafraid to get my hands dirty . . . elbow grease
Give you the shirt off my back, you deserve the best
I'm a one woman man, neglect all the rest
You fresh as a daisy, a sight for sore eyes
Never cease to amaze me . . . together we rise
Because of you I'm full of the joys of spring
So you can be happy, I'll do any and everything

He Died and Made Me GOD Part 7

I'm as happy as a flea in a doghouse
Or a pig getting fat eating slop in a hoghouse
I jumped for joy, then jumped over the moon
I lick my chops, now I'm licking my wounds
The world is my oyster, I'm raring to go
I'm hard like nails . . . Rambo Commando
My actions speak volumes way past loud
Impossible to turn it off or dial it down
I walk around with a smile from ear to ear
My energy is severe and never disappears
7th heaven is where I live . . . gone bananas
Couldn't hold my horses, they ran up the ladder
I'm worked up and just like a dog with two tails
Bouncing off the walls, never fail prevail
I sit down on the earth and kick up my feet
Time to paint the town red, on the edge of my seat

He Died and Made Me GOD Part 8

I'm pre-possessed with the grandfather's paradox
Erase my conception and turn back the clock
All my lights are off, because I live in the dark
Happiness is hard to come by . . . no walk in the park
I eat, sleep and breathe self-murder mutilation
Up my sleeve is death and devastation
I cry for help, but it goes on deaf ears
Can't take a step, many years disappeared
Stolen time, my own throat got cut
Swam against the tide, won't survive . . . a dead duck
A walking disaster, I fell from grace
Landed flat on my face and can't get to 1st base
No riches just rags, I threw in my towel
I swing like Barry Bonds, but everything goes foul
Flied out, grounded out, struck out the end came
No bright side to look at . . . permanent pain

He Died and Made Me GOD Part 9

Time to strike a nerve, I'm a let off some steam
Hit you with the whole ball of wax . . . the God of Everything
Make your skin crawl, get beat black and blue
Here today gone tomorrow is very true
I'm a cut above, hard to gain my trust and love
Your life has no meaning, it's like you never was
I'm a stark raving mad off the rocker type
Knock the daylights out you . . . believe the hype
Pay the price, I'll kill you fair and square
Make you pull out your hair . . . WAR I declare
Seal your fate and live eternity in doom
Etched in stone, I'm light years ahead of you
I don't play with a full deck, it all broke loose
Check my domino effect as I cook your goose
You might as well join me, you can't beat me
I'll take you out nice and neatly . . . discreetly

He Died and Made Me GOD Part 10

I'm about to blow off the cobwebs and reach for the moon
I stop at nothing and move like a typhoon
At all costs, I'm a go great lengths
Sink my teeth into it and be the 1st out the gate
Say die never, hell bent for success
I pound the pavement . . . heroic and fearless
My dreams go beyond the wildest, I buckle down
and hang in there with a frown upside down
Whistles in the dark are music to my ears
I'm in my element whenever cash appears
No time to be in the dumps depressed or dejected
Never looking back, I'm re-made re-connected
I'm going places, all-inclusive vacations
Destinations with my name on the reservations
Everything is God, my style is luxurious
With the luck of the draw I can't lose PERIOD

Hebrews Chapter 11 Verse 1 Part 1

I Am Living Water, Savior, High Priest
The Lamb of God, Servant, Cornerstone Chief
The Bread of Life, Alpha and Omega, True Vine
Light of the World, so I make everything shine
When it comes to peace I'm a Prince
Every time I shoot out blessings . . . guess what? I don't miss
The word that you read is me, I'm a Rock
The door you want to open, all you have to do is knock
I'm the Image of the Invisible God . . . Faithful and True
A Messiah, a Judge, King of the Jews
King of Kings, Lord of Lords, Head of the Church
Bright Morning Star, worship me it works
Almighty Master, Life, Resurrection
The #1 prophet . . . reflection perfection
Believe in me and you've already won
I'm the Most Holy and Only Begotten Son

Hebrews Chapter 11 Verse 1 Part 2

I'm the way, the truth, the life, the creation
Unparalleled, unequal, salvation
Omnipotent, transcendent, infinite
Me coming back to the earth around the corner imminent
Strength and power, remains everlasting
Nothing is above me . . . I'm overstanding
The God of all Gods, Beginning and Ending
I made the universe . . . always extending
Rose of Sharon, Roots of David
I see and know all because of that I'm hated
I will provide, I'm the Great Redeemer
You can't get to where I am unless you a believer
The 1st fruits, Son of God, Son of Man
Everything is destiny . . . a perfect plan
Glorified by the angles, I sacrifice
So you can have eternal life . . . Jesus Christ

Hebrews Chapter 11 Verse 1 Part 3

I was tempted and troubled, so I sweated drops of blood
I give abundant life, I'm the source of love
I cried and slept, was hungry, naked and thirsty
Paid the price for your soul, you don't have to reimburse me
I'm the cure over death, disease and demons
The 9 fruits of the spirit . . . Ephesians
I'm God in the flesh, born sinless
My blessings are unmeasurable, endless
I'm the only perfect person, the perfect God
Unflawed, I stay humble so no need to applaud
Worshipped by angles, died and came back
The rivers dried up, I brought the rain back
Son of the Most High, Heir to all things
Ultimate joy is what I bring and fly with no wings
Judgement Day approaches, only I know the day
Repent and pray . . . it's no other way

Fruit of the Spirit

LOVE lasts forever, the best feeling in existence
Unchanging, unaltered . . . always consistent
JOY comes at a time the sun is ready to rise
When you open your eyes, thank GOD you're alive
PEACE creates no war, mental tranquility
And helps you do what you thought was an impossibility
PATIENCE gives you power to overcome the difficult
And allows you to receive real life miracles
KINDNESS makes your heart warm with generosity
And compassion to treat people with equality
GOODNESS stops you from doing anything bad
Stay focused on the future, instead of living in the past
FAITHFULNESS keeps you devoted and dedicated
Trust the LORD with everything . . . HE'S always celebrated
GENTLENESS brings comfort, no trouble or grief
Inspiration, encouragement, reassurance, relief
SELF-CONTROL produces discipline and self-motivation
Mastery of one's self . . . determination

Medicine Volume 2
The Below Atlantis
Beneath the Abyss Edition

I Could've Never Imagined Part 1

I could've never imagined someone could love me
the way that you do
It's a fact the way I feel, like the sky is blue
Finally I'm treated the way I deserve
All the love I get, I give in return
Together we learn . . . each other's mind and how it works
Because of you, I'm going forward never in reverse
Whatever curse was on my life . . . you lifted it
The happiness you bring, no one could've predicted it
Or scripted it, the perfect movie without a crisis
You was still there for me, when my life was lifeless
Because of that . . . you forever solidified your place
Of being #1, the rest of them erased
Expired, extinct with no traces of
All the women combined can't compare with your love
You're the highest quality, divine, top of the line
1 of a kind, everything about you is mine.

I Could've Never Imagined Part 2

I could've never imagined it would be you to love
and respect me like a god
Don't know why for all the other women it was so hard
I'm satisfied and pleased, my mind is at ease
Whenever together we're strong like Hercules
A megaton bomb, dominant, dynamic
Gigantic, we to Titanic's
So hot you lava-like . . . volcanic
2,000 horsepower full speed undramatic
Where I'm weak you strong, where I'm strong you weak
Supreme team couple, who can't be beat
Never losing, our record is undefeated
Every enemy that came this way retreated
I'm tyrannical, guard my girl at all costs
Other guys took their shot and missed . . . they all lost
Your what I've never had, A-list, high class
Prime quality, the very best, unsurpassed

I Could've Never Imagined Part 3

I could've never imagined that we would make two sons
Let's bring more into the world, my bank account weighs two tons
One by one the whole plan will prevail
Another child born . . . a healthy female
The Lord's ways are mysterious, unimaginable
Unchallengeable, unfathomable
To be blessed with a woman who believes in me
Completely devoted . . . wholeheartedly
Trustworthy, honest and passionate
Ambitious, smart and never blasphemous
Kind and confident, caring, considerate
Complete faithfulness, genuine and generous
I'm the Joker and you Harley . . . Mr. and Mrs. Crook
Creating chaos, breaking every rule in the book
Every other thought it's you I'm thinking of
It's because you're the lady I love

The Fear of Fear Part 1

A black cat crossed my path, so I went the other way
I keep my fingers crossed so I can live another day
I'm not trying to break a mirror or whistle indoors
Bad luck comes in 3's . . . unlucky number 4
6 hundred and 66 got your left hand itching
A owl in your house, death won't be missing
Yellow flowers a curse, so send them back
You jinxed yourself and stepped in dog crap
With the right foot, that's why you never walk backwards
You looked in the mirror too long and your soul got captured
An evil eye you avoid like jumping over a child
Unless you want to stunt their growth . . . unversatile
Haircuts on a Tuesday, a big mistake
You walked under the ladder and sealed your fate
I'm ready to celebrate, drink shots and toast up
But I can't with you . . . it's water in your cup

The Fear of Fear Part 2

If your wife burns a cake on Christmas,
she'll be dead the following year
Don't sing at the dinner table or you'll soon disappear
No bananas on the boat or kissing babies on the lips
You tempted fate, now all your blood drips
Don't cut your nails or chew gum at night
The moment you did, bad luck got an invite
If it's New Year's Eve, leave your clothes uncleaned
Unless you want to have snakes all in your dreams
Three in the morning nightmares, horrible looking creatures
. . . all because you got engaged on Easter
Then pointed to the rainbow in the sky
The wake, the funeral . . . last goodbye's
If you carry a purse, don't let it hit the floor
Or you'll have something negative knocking on your door
Don't open umbrella's indoors, terrible things will increase
Everything gone wrong, Friday the 13th

The Fear of Fear Part 3

Don't play with scissors or stir tea without a spoon
Use your right foot when you enter a room
Bring an old broom to a new house . . . disaster awaits
Evil spirits surround you, because you broke a plate
Dark forces come about when you rock a rocking chair
With nobody in it, tell God your last prayer
Family members slowly start to die off
Now you cursed with an incurable cough
You played with a yo-yo and accidentally hung yourself
It was the wrong decision and your card got dealt
. . . get out of bed the same way you laid in it
Your life is over, finally forever finished
As a gift, never give relatives a knife set
The love is cut . . . just like that
A pregnant woman at a funeral, miscarries the child
Instead of right side up, they buried you facedown

I Found A $100 Bill Part 1

7 hundred and 77, I struck gold
Keep an acorn in your pocket and never grow old
Pray to the goddess of mercy, she'll give you protection
With good health, cure illness and infection
I saw a white elephant and a frog with three legs
A bird dropped a load right on top of your head
Put a bell on your wedding dress, to keep demons away
If you really want to tie the knot, catch the bouquet
I saw two rainbows in the sky, but I didn't point
Make sure you have money for the boatman . . . two coins
Blow breath on the dice every time before you roll them
Give to the poor . . . food, cash and clothing
Say rabbit when you wake up, the month begins
Whenever you hear hunches . . . always listen
Great things come in bunches, expect it to happen
Optimism and good fortune surround the planet

I Found A $100 Bill Part 2

Good things come in two's like twice in a row
When you get married, plant a tree and watch it grow
The 7 luck gods will grant you, a victorious war
Wealth and prosperity . . . I want more
Opportunity was at my door, so I let him in
And he told me success comes from within
A lady bug landed on me, I counted the spots
I played poker after 6 and won the whole pot
Luck fell out of the sky and landed right in my lap
I let the bad of the past go and got rid of all that crap
Instantly I attained increase and gain
No clouds, rain, shame, disdain or pain
Patience, perseverance, hope and guidance
Today I met a fire breathing dragon and formed an alliance
I'm a super-giant, all my dreams came true
Wished upon a star and everything became new

I Found A $100 Bill Part 3

7 days after the full moon, you'll find love at first sight
Take a test with the same pen you studied with last night
Wear new clothes on Easter, keep goldfish around
If you see a 4 leaf clover, pick it up off the ground
Spilling salt is ok, throw it over your left shoulder
Give a Cross or Bible to an infantry soldier
Wear diamonds on Saturdays, keep a key made of gold
If an enemy has a picture of you . . . they have your soul
A penny face up is good luck to the finder
She got a new job, he spilt water behind her
Eat 12 grapes for the New Year's, sleep with a piece
of the wedding cake
Dream about your future spouse . . . first kiss and date
A horseshoe in your house, keeps all the evil out
A swan brings pure love, that's what life is all about
Millionaire status, I'm not hungry I'm famished
So I knock on wood, I want my house to be a palace

Impacted Influences Part 3

Onyx, Coolio, Marvin Gaye
R. Kelly, Babyface, Kid-N-Play
The Fresh Prince, Al Green, Isaac Hayes
Jimi Hendrix, Frankie Beverly and Maze
Mint Condition, New Edition, BBD
Guns-N-Roses, 112, Sheila E
Keith Murray, James Brown, Tyrese
Isley Brothers, Commodores, Dub C
Puffy and Prince, Earth Wind and Fire
Adina Howard, Sade, Mariah
Madonna, Aretha, SWV
Tina Turner, Cindy Lauper, Teena Marie
Toni Braxton, Eurythmics, Rick James
Donna Summer, Diana Ross, Kool and the Gang
Toni Tony Tone, Stevie Wonder, Gladys Knight
Patti LaBelle, George Clinton, Barry White
Craig Mack, Twisted Sister, Boys 2 Men
Blackstreet, Color Me Badd, Van Halen
Usher, Keith Sweat, BB King
Lutha, Jackson 5, Silk, The Supremes
Temptations, Art of Noise, Nice and Smooth
K-Solo, Montell Jordan, Erykah Badu
Diplomats, Genuine, Jodeci
Smokey Robinson, Anita, Whitney
Curtis Mayfield, Spice 1, The O-Jays
Bob Marley, Gerald Levert, Positive K

The God of Evil Part 2

. . . Because you love God, I hate your whole existence
But since I want your soul, never will I keep my distance
I'm in your dreams, waking you up from nightmares
Sweating like you just came out of the sauna . . . never do I fight fair
I'm the one that makes the police kill innocent people
They pigs that transform into weasels
I'm the one that makes a pedophile molest a child
Have them thinking its's ok to do and stay in denial
I'm the one that made you homeless, begging people
for money on the Street
How does it feel, sleeping nights on the concrete?
I'm the one, who made you lose the light bill gambling
Your life I'm damaging, mis-managing, abandoning
I'm the one, who got you drunk so you could cheat on your wife
I'll fix everything, but your soul is my price
I'm the one, who created jealousy, envy and hatred
Its always go be a war, more blood . . . I can taste it
I'm the one that makes murder never have enough kills
To him, it's like stepping on ants . . . a cheap thrill
Never alone, I have millions of demons
I'm evil everyday of every season

Mt. Everest Part 1

To find a man like me . . . you can only hope and wish for
Kill for or be ready to start a war
I'm what you only read about and dream of
You want to make me happy? Get me a thousand machine guns
I prey on predators, nobody in my category
I was made from a different type of laboratory
Unknown to man, I tell no fables
My elements don't exist on the periodic table
Before time began, I was touched by the holiest of hands
To be a top of the food chain hu-man
But more ali-en, I'm not that of man
It'll take you another lifetime to understand
I'm primordial, territorial
I need a statue built to celebrate my memorial
To all the women I supersede any competition
I'm what you have to have, to late you addicted

Mt. Everest Part 2

I'm the best of the best, it's no contest
Compared to me, your ex is a capital F
I'm an A+ come before, stand above all
Every man you've ever been with, was destined to fall
I'm prestigious, resilient, magnificently brilliant
You fell in love with someone who gave unfulfillment
And paid thousands for a wedding that crashed and burned
I told you not to, and showed you the pat-tern
So hopefully you learned, I'm the world's number 1 man
What they can't do I can . . . my plan is grand
Stronger than Superman and Hulk combined
The relationship you was in declined, don't waste your time
And settle for the bottom of the barrel
I'm a natural born god, your boyfriend is a zero
Who cheated on you, lied to you and beat you up
It's a reason why I bat fourth . . . I clean up

Mt. Everest Part 3

I'm there when you need me, never will I fail you
No opinions . . . facts is what I tell you
Sent from heaven, extraordinary input
A real life big shot, Bigfoot
You used to the measly, trivial and trifling
I'm a 5 star czar, 1st place titan
You only deal with the small fry guys, who don't stand for nothing
Opposite of something
Jerkwater, ½ pints, nobody light weights
I'm powerful enough to make them all evaporate
With the snap of a finger, they're no longer visible
Get what you pay for, when you deal with an imbecile
Me on the other hand, I'm aboriginal
Indivisible, invincible
Heavyweight honcho, supremo, colossus
Together . . . it's never anything that can stop us

Ruby Sapphire

10th dimension, my mentality is super strengthened
I'm gone from the reach of comprehension
A week is one day, summer year round
I move around at the speed of sound
A 1,000 times I've been to hell and came back safe
Got kidnapped but escaped . . . 2088
Never been to heaven, but I have land and property there
640 acres . . . eternal trillionaire
Took a vacation to Cloud City, then Atlantis
Mt. Olympus, City of Gold gigantic
Had dinner with Bigfoot, Cyclops and Dracula
Werewolf in London, Predator spectacular
Left the Milky Way and headed straight to Andromeda
Set you on fire, too hot for a thermometer
My energy times my energy times my energy
Plus my power squared . . . slaughters all enemies

The Love Equation

$$\text{GOD}\left(\frac{\text{TRUST}}{\textit{LOVE}}+\frac{\text{COMMITMENT}}{\text{LOVE}}\right)$$

$$=\text{GOD}\left(\frac{\text{ULTIMATE SACRAFICE}}{\text{LOVE}}\right)$$

$$=\text{GOD}\left(\frac{\text{COMPLETE HAPPINESS}}{\text{LOVE}}\right)$$

$$=\text{LONG PROSPEROUS LIFE}$$

Medicine Volume 3
Before the Past, After the Future

10 to the Countless Power Part 1

The Holy Trinity, my daughter
My parents, 3 brothers and sister in that order
Wisdom, understanding, knowledge and college
13 Amendment, slavery abolished
Multiverse, Mega verse, Megatron
Autobahn, Amazon, Babylon
Saigon, Taiwan, Vietnam
Protons, nuetrons, electrons
Octagon, spawn, dawn, Farrakhan
The prize . . . I keep my eyes on
T-i-m-e, the a-i-r
Sun, moon, space, gravity, stars
Earth and fire . . . H-2-O
Food, sleep, shelter, I'm able to grow
Confidence and courage, strength and faith
Sight, smell, sound, touch and taste
I can read and write, unafraid to fight
Afternoon, evening, today, tonight
Up and down, left and right, darkness, light
Orange, blue, yellow, purple, black and white
My poetry, music, freedom and talent
Phone, computer, laptop, tablets
Vacations, a month of relaxation
Blessed to have a foundation of education
Appreciation, of my creation
I worship HIM who gave me salvation

10 to the Countless Power Part 2

Force, energy, velocity, work
Life expert with a thirst to be first
Determination, drive, passion, purpose
Son, brother, great friend and person
Grandson, nephew, super-dad and cousin
The best uncle in existence . . . no discussion
Intelligent with intellect, God-like genetics
Sympathetic, opposite of pathetic
Angelic, Everything Is God authentic
Imagination before Genesis
Concentration, ingeniousness
Physics, chemistry, analytics
Probability of statistics . . . I'm gifted
And blessed with a brain, heart, lungs and liver
Eyes to see, the 18th of November
Kidneys, skin, bones, teeth
Hair on my head, my soul is beneath
I can add, subtract, multiply and divide
My body won't quit, I'm built to survive
Love, liberty, life, freedom, equality
Astrology, justice, geometry
Thank God for laughter and comedy
Monogamy, the process of psychology
Alpha male, never fail . . . prevail
I'm destined for heaven never will I see hell

Because I'm Sober Part 1

BECAUSE I'M SOBER, I can get up and go to the job
without a hangover
And not stay in bed and let the day passover
Alcohol is my odor, smell me from a mile away
A 12 pack and a pint of E and J
BECAUSE I'M SOBER, my paranoia stays under control
The weed got me blowed, breathing smoke out of my nose
Thought I had a conversation with my soul
. . . Can't eat without my eyes being closed
BECAUSE I'M SOBER, if the police pull me over
They wouldn't smell anything, but new truck aroma
No sobriety test, I keep my composure
No breathalyzer, so I keep rolling
BECAUSE I'M SOBER, my liver can finally be fixed
Brain cells can stop dying, old habits get kicked
My kidneys, flush my body out with a thorough rinse
A strong heart is at the top of the list
BECAUSE I'M SOBER, I stay out of the liquor store
. . . They know my face when I come thru the door
A preferred customer at the counter is my usual
I play the lottery instead . . . no funerals

Because I'm Sober Part 2

BECAUSE I'M SOBER, my face looks like the hand of God touched it
We had a long conversation and discussed it
I had to make some life changing adjustments
I'm convinced of what He tells me, His word is trusted
BECAUSE I'M SOBER, I can sleep well like a baby
Fresh out of the womb, 10 hours daily
My pillow feels softer, rapid eye movement
Body got stronger, nothing but improvement
BECAUSE I'M SOBER, I got more time to write
Less time to get into a brawl and fight
Or verbally assault somebody, my tongue is murderous
I'm kool and don't become merciless
BECAUSE I'M SOBER, I have more energy
More brain power, more memory
Too much Mary Jane got me slow mentally
. . . I'm trying to live another century
BECAUSE I'M SOBER, I have an extra $250 a month
I buy my daughter more things and can take her to lunch
Cigarettes and beer, alcohol and weed
Cost me enough, my goal is succeed

I Looked into My Future

Everything I ever asked for I received
I'm unbelievably rich, beyond anything I can dream
My face is famous, my name is household
My work is worth more than diamonds and gold
Rare like red bananas, a green moon
A clear glass grand piano, my reflection is two
I'm at the Super Bowl and NBA Championships
. . . No number big enough for what my passion is
My mansion is, worth about 10 mil
My family will never have to worry about bills
College is paid for, I'm wealthy and loaded
Everything you hear and read from me I wrote it
Devoted . . . it took one person to notice
Now I'm everywhere, popularity exploded

All-Powerful

I give hope to the hopeless, love to the hateful
Appreciation to the ungrateful
Inspiration to the uninspired
Sight for the blind, jobs to the fired
Hearing for the deaf, shelter for the homeless
Help for the helpless, a phone for the phoneless
Food for the hungry, richness to the poor
An atheist . . . a sav-ior

I give sobriety for the intoxicated
Encouragement to the frustrated
Euphoria if you depressed, blessings for the cursed
Faith to the doubtful, water for your thirst
Happiness to the miserable, health for the sick
. . . Perseverance to anyone who wants to quit
Strength for the powerless, freedom for the chained
Intelligence to the foolish, relief for the pain

I give fitness to the overweight, hair to the bald
Delightfulness to the angry, righteousness to the wrong
Non-violence to the violent, repairs for the broken
Any closed door will become open
Clues for the clueless, knowledge to the ignorant
Humbleness for the inconsiderate
Respect for the respectless, peace for the war-like
If you in the darkness, I'll give you more light

I Know Everything Part 1

I know where space ends and begins
I have documentation of how deep the ocean really is
I know why we lose and why we win
I know exactly where I'm going and where I've been
And the reasons my best friend went to the pen
We got in trouble every time drinking juice and gin
Where does evil come from, suicide and sin?
Trespasses always start within the within
What's the date of your death, what time and where?
Do you really want to know the truth, or are you to scared?
Knowledge is the greatest power one can possess
I'm happily married to wisdom, who I'll never re-lin-quish
Where does all the good come from, who made the pyramids?
What would make someone not want to take care of their kids?
Cold cases become hot, unsolved murders get solved
After 50 years the bones are buried . . . flesh is gone
I know who created God and how we got here
I know exactly what you afraid of and everything you fear
All questions have answers, nothing is a mystery
It's a cure for cancer . . . aids has a remedy

I Know Everything Part 2

I saw a future that was unseen
And went back in the past to live again when I was 17
Dreams and nightmares have meaning . . . what do they mean?
Thoughts your brain can't begin to conceive
Jack the Ripper, Bermuda Triangle
I wish you was a fly on the wall, when I talk to the angels
The Zodiac Letters finally get decoded
Aliens come to the earth with a motive
Time is an illusion, but gravity is real
Because of greed and money . . . blood spills
You're never getting married, so stay off the dating sights
Take my advice, stop wasting time and do more with your life
I have the coordinates to Atlantis, Loch Ness Monster
His dad wasn't in his life, so he grew up to be a mobster
You can't break an egg when it's already broken
Quit now or in 10 years . . . die from smoking
Blood red waterfalls, Vatican secrets
It's nothing that can compare to my uniqueness
Dark matter, dark energy equals a poltergeist
I know what's faster than the speed of light

Set You on Fire Part 1

I'm one of the greatest poets ever in life
I'll smash your hands into a million pieces . . .
never again will you write
No tongue, so you can't talk, read out loud, or recite
My words hit you like uppercuts, from a Tyson fight
I'm a two-legged hyena, my laugh is villainous
My life is rigorous . . . carnivorous
What I say is the highest law like the book of Leviticus
I'm the anti-version of your illiterate ignorance
Your whole and complete soul is worthlessness
Everything you've ever done in life was purposeless
I'll shatter and blood splatter you, because you delicate
I left the crime scene with no clues of evidence
Blame your parents for being born without intelligence
I blame mine for being born a perfectionist
Every time I see you, I see rat excrement
I'm excellent, when I make it rain . . . I rain pestilence
Take my time and skin you alive down to your skeleton
It's like you was never born . . . no relevance
I won't stop with you, disappear all your relatives
Everything Is God . . . Chief Executive

Set You on Fire Part 2

I'm a hall of fame poet, ultimate writer
You radiate like the sun, but I shine 10 million times brighter
I'm a tiger on the loose . . . searching for victims
I'm vindictive, pillaging people like you is addictive
I'll destroy your soul, let satan have total control
. . . Burn for eternity is the goal
Lake of fire torture, I'll let you leave
When you see demons eating popsicles and ice cream
Until then . . . you can scald in the heat
Keep watching me, I'm a ball in the street
My mind deepens, I get stronger you weaken
Try as hard as you like . . . I cannot be beaten
But I'll beat you to death, then I'll beat out your brains
Bloodstains, throw you out the plane
Explode like a egg when you hit the ground . . . feel no pain
This poem is a freight train that's unstoppable
With a full head of steam . . . I'm unconquerable
My whole point is to blow you to bits
Because you're less than nothing, your nothingness

My Result of Combining Letters

My words **ALLOW** you to have freedom, you never would've had
You can't live without them, it's what you have to have
My words **BLESS**, with nothing less than success
Believe you the best, keep your mind fresh and progress
My words **BRING** energy, equivalent to the sun
27,000,000 degrees, burn anything . . . anyone
My words **CURE**, restore and revive
Your mind is forever alive, from sunset to sunrise
My words **GIVE** you power with the strength of a grizzly bear
And courage to become a multi-millionaire
My words **HELP** you fear God, listen to His message
Learn lessons, He'll take away all of your stresses
My words **INSPIRE**, ignite and force
You to go forth, in you is the source
My words **MAKE** your imagination
go to every possible dimension
Beyond human comprehension, another universe invented
My words **SHOW** you the light, you've lived without for so long
The opposite of darkness, a thousand years strong
My words **TEACH**, educate, indoctrinate
Now you possess the skills to concentrate . . . so dominate

2,000 Words

Power, energy, force, strength
Might, muscle, vivaciousness
Unrelenting, unpretending, unending
Everything Is God . . . forever trending
Triumph, victory, slaughter, surpass
Conquer, crush, prevail, advance
Dedication, devotion, sacrifice
Blessings, happiness, joy, life
Christ, Messiah, Lord, Master
Son of the living God . . . green pastures
Paradise, perfection, cloud 9, direction
Pure protection, death, resurrection
Re-connection, re-conception, re-live
Exonerate, vindicate, forgive
Untouched, unused, unconfused
Foundation improved . . . gratitude
Rejoice, relish, revel, savor
Respect, admiration, re-think behavior
Gold, cash, fortune, cream
Abundantly rich, a real dream

Love has No Color

You don't like me because of the color of my skin?
But unseen to you is the great person that lives within
My instincts are built-in, to never be a has-been
And you would dis-like me even more . . . if I had a twin
Judging me is a sin, I'm free like the wind
I'm not a jailbird or a loser, because I don't lose I win
Your whole evaluation of me is wrong and your analysis
I'm brilliant, sharp, super smart and talented
I was taught to have morals, values, ethics and decency
My happiness comes frequently, I live peacefully
I stay away and far from trouble, nothing illegally
Me showing kindness to others comes easily
Ingeniously . . . magnificently
I came to the realization, every day is a gift to me
No one is better than anyone, all blood is red
Don't make a negative change, but a positive one instead

Not That of Man Everything is God

Less Than 1% Part 1

If less than 1% of illiterate people learned how to read and write
There would be more of a chance for them to succeed in life
Jobs and opportunities give a purpose to function
Become something instead of nothing . . . produce production.
If less than 1% of people stayed out of jail
More families could win, triumph, and prevail
They build penitentiaries before they build colleges.
A billion dollar a year business of bondages.
If less than 1% of people ate healthy and changed their diet
More people could live longer and stop dying
From high blood pressure, heart attacks and strokes
Type 1 and 2 diabetes is no joke.
If less than 1% of people got free from drug addiction
More dreams can be followed with no restriction
No cocaine or pain killers, crack, or heroin
You clean now, so it's like night and day . . . no comparison.
If less than 1% of people could love themselves
There would be more room for greatness to excel
Love is never second, but always first
If more of us tried . . . we could have heaven on earth.

Less Than 1% Part 2

If less than 1% of the police stopped shooting
and killing innocent human beings
More years could be lived instead of used to grieve
People who look like me get assassinated first
Operation depopulation . . . we get it the worse
If less than 1% of fathers actually took care of their child
More children would go to bed and wake up feeling proud
And their lives won't be damaged or ruined for decades to come
They feel protection and love . . . get trained how not to be a bum
If less than 1% of people stop committing suicide
At least one person out of a million would still be alive
Depression, despair, and hopelessness would all pass
The happiness inside of you overpowers the sad
If less than 1% of the population didn't live in poverty
½ of the people in the world could touch and taste quality
More children could grow up instead of dying from starvation
Malnutrition, inadequate sanitation . . . dehydration
If less than 1% of missing people suddenly reappeared
More families can rejoin and comeback together after years
No tears just smiles, hugs and kisses
Birthday wishes . . . presents on Christmas

Will the Day Ever Come

Will it ever be 1 second, 1 minute, 1 hour, 1 day, 1 year
When there is no violence?
Will the day ever come when we don't have thoughts of impurity?
But have confidence to never feel insecurity
No more immaturity we born with a grown-up mentality
Intelligent enough to not be tricked into believing
christopher columbus discovered america . . . that's a fallacy
Will the day ever come when all the homeless in
The world get a nice home to live
With soap, hot water and relax with the air conditioned?
Toothpaste and clothes, food in the refrigerator
Even if the power goes out they got a backup generator
Will the day ever come when the police get convicted
And sentenced to do time . . . for killing, murdering, slaughtering,
And causing innocent blood to shed and get punished for their crime?
To me the saddest thing is that the color of my skin makes me an automatic threat
You already despise me, detest me, and we never even met
Will the day ever come when I don't have to worry
About crime and live to be 26 years old without being killed
By my own kind? That's ½ the battle I
Still have to fight against time, so I don't
Waste it, but make it and take back what's mine

Conceived in the Brain, Born in the Mind

I speak like no other . . . because every time I get on stage I'm like a wild animal let loose out of the cage. Some of you will have never seen or heard of me before, but I guarantee you will never forget what you about to get from me. Everything is God, now that name is forever embedded into your memory . . . infused, unmoved and stuck in your memory. Until the end of infinity I'm who you cannot forget, so from this day until the last day your heart stops beating, you always go remember me. My words and your brain have finally come together like a sperm and egg . . . fertilization has occurred. I got the password to your soul now, I got control now, I'm a do everything in my power to give you all of my know-how. I'm a long term recollection, my reflection will never leave the mecca of your minds thoughts like a disease with no cure. The perfection of my personality is infectious and is spreading in all directions above and below the equator. Before long . . . all will be impregnated, drenched and drowned, soaked and saturated with my intellectual injections, until the end of actuality and creation is no more.

1st Class Overnight Mail to Hell Part 1

I'm writing this long overdue letter because I'm at my wits end of you and all of your crap, schemes, tricks, lies, and all of the other evilisms that you try and do to ruin my life. I know you hate me and I know I disgust you because I believe in the Lord God. I am filled with the Holy Spirit and the True Love of God my Father. I will continue to rebuke you to get behind me every day. If God hates you then so do I, because I am what He is. My life will continue to be blessed beyond anything humanly possible from now until the Lord comes back and takes me with Him to Heaven. What you have tried to do to me has not turned my faith from God, but only made me stronger in Him. I don't like you at all and if it was up to me you and all you represent would be gone from this planet. I know that you don't want me alive so that I can be a messenger of God to spread His word across the globe. If I have to rebuke you a million times a day I will because I am tired and literally sick of you and your hideous ways. I am not afraid of you or your demons and evil does not have any POWER over me including my mind, body, or soul. Your time is nearing and as much as you know about my future . . . I know about yours too. While you laugh at me I don't laugh back because it does me no good. I focus my vengeance thru the Lord and allow Him to do His work while I look from the sideline and keeping my (POM) peace of mind.

Holistically,
God's Child

Can and Cannot

You can take all my sadness, grief and gloom
But you cannot take my joy
You can take all my madness, doubt and doom
But you cannot take what I enjoy

You can take all my misery and bad behavior
But you cannot take my passion
You can take all my injuries, violent ways and anger
But you cannot take my compassion or anything I imagine

You can take all my guilt, fear and frustration
But you cannot take working out or lifting weights
You can take all my shame, tears, impatience
But you cannot take the talent I possess . . . I'm great

You can take everything I hate, my faults and flaws
But you cannot take my courage and confidence
You can take the voices in my head, they want me
to kill you all.
But you cannot take my peace of mind or consciousness

You can take all the pressure, aggravation and stress
But you cannot take He that is in me . . . I rise above
You can take all my transgressions, unhappiness
But you cannot take my power, my soul, or my love

Kitchen or the Bedroom

You got a knife to your neck, a gun in your mouth
You chose not to listen, so I'm takin you out
I guess you didn't know me well enough . . . not to force my hand
Nowhere for you to go, but to no man's land
I'm a hit you where it hurt, right where you deserve
Destroy your whole system network of nerves
No messages sent to the brain or spinal cord
So you won't even feel the pain, bleed out on the floor
It's my face you see, the poltergeist in your nightmares
I'm dreadful, fearful . . . I don't fight fair
Electric chair, gas chamber, firing squad
Now you can meet your maker, the opposite of God
You thought you was going to heaven? satan waiting for you
Dress light . . . tank tops, shorts and house shoes
You can't defend where I attack, start your car it blows up
Or get found in your bathtub on your back nose up

Touch Success

I have a beautiful wife and children, with more money I can count
A state of the art 5-bath, 10 bedroom house
My refrigerator stay full, I got clothes and cars
Slim to none was my chances, but I beat the odds
Everything is God . . . with diamonds, gold and works of art
At one point my life was dying so I had to restart
100 acres of my own island, I pull up in a yatch
With my real family and friends . . . a vacation spot
And it's not all about the physical, but more of what you can't touch
Mentally get a victory, defeat gets crushed
Spiritually and psychologically . . . win methodically
You can accomplish anything, self-fulfill your own prophecy
And get close enough so you can smoke the cigar
Never forget who and whose you are
Live and breathe success, snatch the achievement
You can do all things if you believe it

3,000 Words

Failure, disappointment, frustration
Unconnected, alone, isolation
Meaningless, valueless, worthless
Fail, of no avail, no purpose
Joylessness, torment, heartache
Unhappiness, hardship, heartbreak
Hurt, discomfort, excruciated pain
Permanent rain, typhoon, hurricane
Cursed, afflicted, vile, wretched
Wrong, rotten, evil, respectless
Forgiveness, mercy, redemption
Super strengthen, ascension, 10th dimension
Peacefulness, calm, tranquility
Everything is God and Trinity
Serenity, healthy physically
A divine trilogy, infinitely
Blessed, privileged, fortunate
Heaven sent, resourcefulness
Master, All-Knowing, All-Seeing
Father God, Creator, Supreme Being

Everything I Hate

I hate what God hate and He hates the wicked
And those who do evil will not be acquitted
I hate the police, they kill my kind and get away
Revenge will be sweet, every pig has his day
I hate liars and thieves, to them it's a routine
It's nothing you can ever say to me that I'll believe
I hate pedophiles who prey on the innocent
They should never get out of jail . . . life imprisonment
I hate people who hate my people, or think they born superior
Every person's blood is red, so don't judge my exterior
I hate people who can't drive or go slow in the fast lane
Statistically you will create accidents, death and pain
I hate the fact the world revolves around money
Trying to get it turns bloody and ends ugly
I hate the devil most of all, he's the cause
And everybody is effected . . . fight and stay strong

I'm Possessed

I'm possessed because I'm extremely blessed
With so many reasons to live, I choose life over death
The God of all Gods has control of my movements
International, supernatural improvements
Advancements, enhancements . . . His voice tells me
commandments
I did what I was told and got gigantic finances
He dominates everything I do
Everything I say, everything I dreamed came true
The power He fills me with I take on . . . embrace
My Spirit has it clenched and gripped, so it can't escape
Will never escape, I'm draped with the purest blood
Even if I'm hated by every human being on the face
of the earth, I'm who
My God will still love
He lives and breathes through me, my body is a vessel
I have authority over demons and devils . . . I'm successful
Greater is He that is in me, the One you can't see
I'm a spitting image of His Excellency

About the Author

Marvin O'Neal was born on November 18, 1974, to two strong-willed, blue-collar, hard-working parents. Being able to verbalize and talk by ten months old made him very articulated, opinionated, and vocal.

In the Spring of 1997, he took on the name "Everything" because God is everything who created, blessed, and instilled in him everything that He is. Since that time, there have been hundreds of poems, rap lyrics, script concepts and ideas, plus countless upon countless thoughts written from the deepest realms of his mind.

His life has been a mammoth roller coaster of 1,000-feet drops, dark abyss-like tunnels, and endless corkscrew turns. By faith and making ultimate sacrifices for God the Father, Holy Spirit and Son . . . Everything is God became conceived and born.

Made in the USA
Lexington, KY
10 November 2019

56798401R00085